Are Cops Only Shooting People Like Me?

Are Cops Only Shooting People Like Me?

Stan Campbell

D.O.P.E

DE-ESCALATING OFFICER PATROL ENCOUNTERS · THE MOVEMENT ·

ARE COPS ONLY SHOOTING PEOPLE LIKE ME?
Published by Coach, Speak & Serve
Copyright © 2018 Stanley Campbell

Printed in the United States of America

ISBN: 978-0-998-7829-4-2

Special discounts are available on bulk quantity purchases by book clubs, associations and special interest groups. For details, email support@coachspeakserve.com.com or call (800) 930-1895.

For information, go to www.dopethemovement.com/books.

DEDICATION

This book is dedicated to our youth and the "Village,"
who are the children, parents, professionals, and police
officers across the nation. I believe de-escalation is a shared
responsibility between the citizen and the officer (50/50), so
we should all be trained to have the best and safest outcome.

ACKNOWLEDGMENTS

I want to thank my family, business partners, and friends who support my "purpose" projects.

Thanks to my parents, Mona and Clifton, for encouraging your children to work hard in everything we do, ask questions of what we don't understand, and challenge injustice.

Thanks to my D.O.P.E. the Movement advisors, Don West, Donna Hicks Izzard, Dr. Alexis Artwohl, Dr. Pamela Wiley, and Det. John "Rob" High, for keeping me focused and sharing your words of wisdom.

Thanks to my sister, Tisha Campbell-Martin, for being the first person to ask me to create police encounter material to share on social media.

Thanks to my Brand Manager, Aprille Franks-Hunt, who refused to allow D.O.P.E. to just be a "Moment" and pushed for me to turn it into a "Movement." Thank you to her awesome team for assisting me with creating and polishing my brand.

Thanks to my Spectrum Shield partner, Dr. Pamela Wiley, for her support and work. This program, partnered with D.O.P.E., is designed to teach young men with autism how to make police encounters safe.

Thanks to my children, Mikaela and Devin, for growing into amazing adults and using what I've taught them during their encounters with law enforcement.

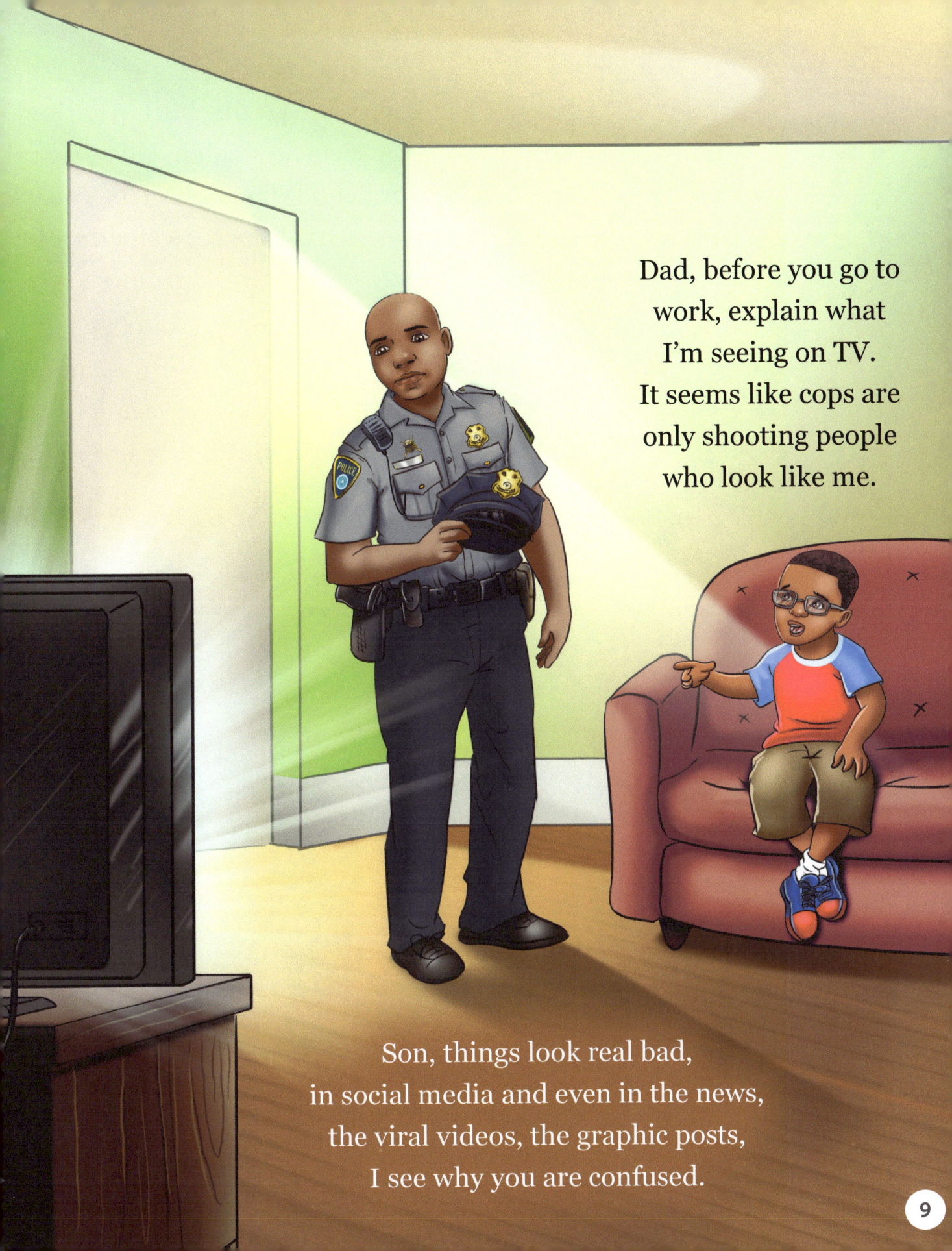

Dad, before you go to work, explain what I'm seeing on TV. It seems like cops are only shooting people who look like me.

Son, things look real bad,
in social media and even in the news,
the viral videos, the graphic posts,
I see why you are confused.

Yes Dad, can it get much worse?
People are getting hurt over things
that seem so small by those we call
for help. What's going on, can we
trust the cops at all?

Son, most cops are good across the
nation, close to a million answer the call.
They do great work, they serve and
protect, and they know they're not
above the law.

POLICE

But Dad, I see protests and a lot of people with their hands high in the air; and signs that say "I Can't Breathe," "Please Don't Shoot Me," and that police don't care.

Son, it's always tragic. Emotions are high, people get angry, and tensions rise. Any bad shooting is one too many, and public outrage is no surprise.

11

But Dad, the man in New York? It was five against one, and over selling cigarettes—he lost his life. And that man on Facebook Live who got shot in front of his daughter and his wife?

De-escalation must increase, Son. Things are getting out of hand. More less-lethal options and community programs should also be part of the plan.

Well Dad, it doesn't seem fair, like Tamir with the
toy gun; even people without weapons die!
You always say cops need more training,
but is racism really why?

JUSTICE FOR TAMIR

REVOLUTION NOTHING

Son, race relations in this nation truly have
a struggled past. But police officers with
less training, I am maintaining, pull the
trigger much too fast.

JUSTICE FOR TAMIR

Dad, I'm angry for them. It seems there's no
justice, as the hashtag list grows long.
Cops don't get punished, it's so confusing,
like saying they've done nothing wrong.

It's case by case, Son. Some are found
guilty if they use excessive force.
There's an investigation, a court, and a jury
a decision rendered, and jail, of course.

But Dad, what if I'm accused and I didn't do what the officer said? What if the officer is unprofessional or uses bad language, or I know my rights are not read?

Son, just comply. During the stop is not the time to make your side known. There are supervisors to complain later. Your only job is to get home.

Dad, I'm gonna share this info with my friends on the Internet and in school, about giving respect, making it safe for both sides, and how de-escalation is cool.

That's right, Son, each should do their part and care for the other—yes, it's true— check their ego, be compliant, and move slowly when they do.

I'm proud to be your son, and thank you, Dad, for all that you do.
All I know is when I grow up, I want to be a good cop, just like you!

POLICE

SPECIAL THANKS

I would like to give special thanks to all the police departments that adopt community policing as a philosophy and those who have increased training courses in de-escalation.

Thanks to all those who work in P.A.L. and D.A.R.E. programs and other unique community relations collaborative projects.

A very special thanks to those officers who stand in the light to represent their departments in a positive manner and those who give extra time and effort to "bridge the gap" between citizens and police. Here are a few that we support below:

- Chief Joseph Paulino (SBUSD PD) with the Learn 2 Live Community Forum Initiative
- Major C. Huth (KCMO PD) with the Unleashing the Power of Unconditional Respect Initiative
- Lt. Wayland Cubit (OCPD) with the Family Awareness and Community Teamwork Program
- Officer Tommy Norman (Little Rock, Arkansas PD) with his Positive Community Policing Initiative
- Officer Deon Joseph (LAPD – Skid Row Division) with the Just Like You Mentoring Program
- Officer Billy Ray Fields (Ocilla, Georgia PD) with the Squad Up and Good Cops Initiatives
- Officer Jennifer Maddox (Chicago PD) with the nonprofit Future Ties Community Program
- Officer Lamar Sharpe (Canton, OH PD) with the Be a Better Me Initiative

ABOUT THE AUTHOR

Use-of-Force Expert, Social Activist, and Speaker Stan Campbell is the COO of CCW Safe, a national legal defense membership organization for licensed concealed weapon carriers. Stan is known for his teaching experience as a law enforcement instructor and has personally trained over four thousand uniformed officers and criminal justice professionals across the nation in the proper use of force, defensive tactics, and how to de-escalate potentially violent encounters. He has won valor awards, led tactical and street crime teams, and is renowned by many for his passion for public service, his expertise in police encounters, and his impeccable sense of character and integrity in his life and work. But he simply sees himself as a man ignited by a mission—to build a stronger bridge between law enforcement and the communities they serve.

Born in the tumultuous inner city of Newark, New Jersey, Stan grew up in a poor, often violent, neighborhood. His first step toward his life's calling was his work as an Emergency Medical Technician in that same area, serving alongside police officers in the streets to make a difference. In that role, he began to take dutiful note of the ever-growing gap that violence created between communities and police. The aftermath of countless shootings and murders was etched on his spirit—forever. Honoring his desire to step toward his higher purpose, he enrolled in the police academy. That step sparked a lifelong commitment to public service. Over the course of twenty years, Stan's illustrious and honored career in law enforcement would take him from patrol officer to lieutenant, from the Street Crimes Unit to Sniper Tactical Unit (SWAT), and as far as the Caribbean to protect, serve, and teach, all the while searching his soul for what he should do next.

That next step was to stand up and speak out—for officers, for citizens, and for a nation weighted by violence, strained race relations, and uncertainty.

Every case, every first response, and every officer-involved shooting widened his lens on the dynamics between law enforcement and the people they serve, particularly young people in disadvantaged communities. Stan knew it was his calling to be a catalyst for change in his community and, soon, the nation.

Today, he strives to be an informed voice who can build a bridge between the public and police officers, humanizing both sides and, ultimately, creating a critical dialogue that can lead to less violent encounters.

Led by his passion, fueled by this purpose, and prepared by his experience, Stan is uniquely positioned to expand the dialogue between officers and citizens. He tackles the task from two familiar angles—training and service. He recently introduced D.O.P.E. (De-escalating Office Patrol Encounters), a comprehensive training and awareness program sharing industry tips and personal training advice to citizens and police officers simultaneously. Stan also plans to lend his expertise to communities to promote peaceful protest and partnerships between citizen groups and law enforcement agencies.

Devoted to eradicating the myths, miscommunication, and misconceptions that take lives instead of saving them, Stan Campbell is a voice for justice, for fairness, and for the protection of lives—everywhere.

ATTENTION PARENTS –
JOIN THE MOVEMENT

**Please take our free pledge
of de-escalation at**

WWW.DOPETHEMOVEMENT.COM

*D.O.P.E. is a fiscally sponsored program
with Social Good Fund, a 501(c)3 organization*

www.ingramcontent.com/pod-product-compliance
Lightning Source LLC
Chambersburg PA
CBHW042015090426

42811CB00015B/1654